BLACK

By Patricia M. Stockland
Illustrated by Julia Woolf

Content Consultant
Susan Kesselring, MA
Literacy Educator and Preschool Director

magic
wagon

visit us at www.abdopublishing.com

Published by Magic Wagon, a division of the ABDO Publishing Group, 8000 West 78th Street, Edina, Minnesota 55439. Copyright © 2009 by Abdo Consulting Group, Inc. International copyrights reserved in all countries. All rights reserved. No part of this book may be reproduced in any form without written permission from the publisher.

Looking Glass Library™ is a trademark and logo of Magic Wagon.

Printed in the United States.

Text by Patricia M. Stockland
Illustrations by Julia Woolf
Edited by Jill Sherman
Interior layout and design by Nicole Brecke
Cover Design by Nicole Brecke

Library of Congress Cataloging-in-Publication Data

Stockland, Patricia M.
  Black / by Patricia M. Stockland ; illustrated by Julia Woolf.
     p. cm. — (Colors)
  ISBN 978-1-60270-255-4
  1. Black—Juvenile literature. 2. Color—Juvenile literature. I. Woolf, Julia, ill. II. Title.
  QC495.5.S77 2009
  535.6—dc22
                        2008001604

I help my sister pack the car.

The car is black.

4

I see cars on the road.

The tires are black.

We find the dirt path.

The path is black.

8

12

The bird sees a tasty bug.

The bug is black.

I see a big bird in a tree.

The bird is black.

My sister lays down the blanket.

The blanket stripes are black.

We look through the telescope.

The telescope is black.

We eat gumdrops under the stars.

The gumdrops are black.

My sister gives me her warm coat.

The coat is black.

19

I stroke my sister's soft hair.

Her hair is black.

What Is Black?

There are three primary colors: red, blue, and yellow. These colors combine to create other colors. All three primary colors mixed together make black. You can also mix black with other colors to make them darker.

Primary Colors

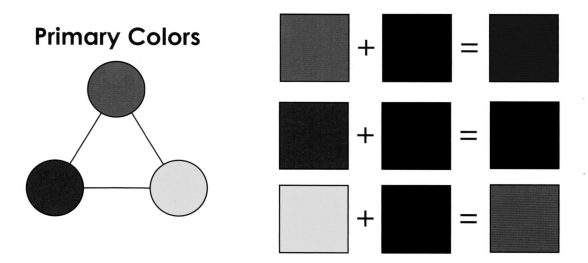

What black things did you see in the story?

Words to Know

blanket—a soft, warm covering.

gumdrop—a type of candy that is chewy and sweet.

stripe—a band of color.

telescope—a tool that helps you see things that are very far away.

tire—the rubber part of a wheel.

Web Sites

To learn more about the color black, visit ABDO Publishing Company on the World Wide Web at **www.abdopublishing.com**. Web sites about the colors are featured on our Book Links page. These links are routinely monitored and updated to provide the most current information available.

D1071268